W9-CEJ-100

German fighter aircraft

French soldier's uniform

British Whippet tank

Turkish medal

Can with hidden messages

Woman working in a factory

Hammer and sickle badge

3

Taking sides

By 1914, Europe's strongest nations had split into two rival groups. On one side were France, Britain, and Russia. On the other was Germany, with Austria-Hungary, and the Ottoman Empire of Turkey. Each side had big armies, and new weapons.

Germany's kaiser had power to order war.

Kaiser Wilhelm II

Germany and Britain had been friendly in the past. But now Germany's emperor, Kaiser Wilhelm II, was ready for war. Wilhelm II saw Britain, France, and Russia as enemies trying to stop Germany from having too much power.

FACT FILE

» **Central Powers**
Siding with Germany were the empires of Austria-Hungary and Ottoman Turkey. They were both weaker than Germany. Together, these three were called the Central Powers.

Germany

Austria-Hungary

Ottoman Turkey

Balkan unrest

In 1912–13, wars broke out in the Balkans, an area in southeast Europe. Here, Serbia, Greece, Montenegro, and Bulgaria fought to end Ottoman (Turkish) rule in the region.

Balkan wars
The Balkan wars weakened the power of the Ottoman Empire, and made Russia and Germany greater rivals.

A band of fighters in the Balkans

The tsar believed he alone ruled Russia.

Britain's king had little power over plans for war.

Nicholas II and George V

George V of Britain and Nicholas II of Russia each ruled vast empires. They were cousins and looked alike. In 1913, they visited another cousin, Kaiser Wilhelm II of Germany. The family meeting did not prevent war in 1914.

FACT FILE

» Allies
Britain and France had been enemies in past wars, but they became allies against Germany's growing power. They were joined by Russia.

Britain	France	Russia

Arms race

The struggle for power led to an "arms race" (building up of armaments, or weapons) between nations. This was helped by advances in technology and new factory methods. Both sides competed to build more guns and ships.

German arms factory
The Krupp factory made guns that could fire shells 7 miles (12 km) away.

British battleship
HMS *Dreadnought* (1906) was the first modern battleship. It had huge guns.

The assassination

Franz Ferdinand was in a car with his wife, Sophie, when both were shot dead. The shootings shocked Europe. Austria, with German support, decided to punish Serbia. On July 28, 1914, Austria went to war with Serbia.

War begins

A shooting started World War I. On June 28, 1914, Archduke Franz Ferdinand, heir to Austria-Hungary's empire, visited Sarajevo in Bosnia. Bosnia had been part of Austria-Hungary since 1908. Ferdinand was assassinated (killed) by a Bosnian Serb, who wanted freedom from Austrian rule. Austria-Hungary blamed Serbia for the killing and declared war.

Austrians march

Troops from Austria-Hungary marched off to attack Serbia. Because Russia supported Serbia, Russian armies also got ready for battle.

3 German armies gather

Germany told Russia to stop its armies. Russia said no. So on August 1, 1914, Germany declared war on Russia. Germany also planned to attack France.

In the war's first year, more than **2 million men** in Britain volunteered to fight.

France gets ready

France was Russia's ally, so on August 3, France went to war with Germany. Posters told French soldiers and sailors to prepare for battle.

ARMÉE DE TERRE ET ARMÉE DE MER

ORDRE
DE MOBILISATION GÉNÉRALE

Britain joins in

Germany planned to attack France by marching through Belgium. Britain promised to help Belgium, so from August 4, British troops joined the war.

Key players

Europe's leading nations, along with the US, Canada, Australia, and peoples in the Middle East, India, and Africa took part in the war. On one side was a group of countries called the Central Powers. On the other side were the Allies.

The Central Powers

Germany was the leader of the Central Powers. Other nations in this alliance were Austria-Hungary, Bulgaria, and the Ottoman, or Turkish, Empire.

FRANZ JOSEPH
Austria-Hungary

Emperor Franz Joseph I (1830–1916) ruled Austria-Hungary. His government wanted Serbia punished after a Serbian shot dead the emperor's nephew and heir in 1914. This led Austria-Hungary to war.

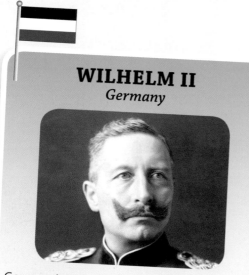

WILHELM II
Germany

Germany's Kaiser (emperor) Wilhelm (1859–1941) was a grandson of Britain's Queen Victoria and cousin of Britain's King George V. However, Wilhelm believed Britain stood in the way of Germany becoming a world power.

MEHMED V
Ottoman Empire

Sultan Mehmed V (1844–1918) ruled the Ottoman Empire. However, power was held by General Enver Pasha, who took Germany's side. After the war, Mehmed's brother was the last Turkish sultan.

The Allies

Russia went to help Serbia in 1914, and Britain and France backed them. Other Allies included Belgium, Italy, Japan, US, and the British Empire.

GEORGES CLEMENCEAU
France

Clemenceau (1841–1929) was prime minister of France from 1917. Known as "The Tiger," he led France to victory. Clemenceau pushed for harsh peace terms to punish Germany for war damage.

NICHOLAS II
Russia

Tsar Nicholas (1868–1918) was a cousin of Britain's George V. Russia's tsars ruled with complete power, but Nicholas's empire fell apart. A poor war leader, he was overthrown in the 1917 Revolution.

WOODROW WILSON
United States

President Wilson (1856–1924) kept the US out of the war until 1917. He hoped for a lasting peace after the war and helped set up the League of Nations, so that nations could work together to prevent wars in the future.

DAVID LLOYD GEORGE
Britain

David Lloyd George (1863–1945) was in government at the start of the war and masterminded Britain's war effort, helping to increase the production of weapons. He became prime minister in 1916, and played a big part in the peace talks of 1919.

Off to war

There had not been a big European war since the 1870s. So when World War I started in the summer of 1914, no one knew what it would be like. Plans for the war were mostly based on old ideas. Many new soldiers were sure the war would be over by Christmas.

REALLY?

Boys as young as **14 lied about their age** so they could join the army. They were supposed to be **18**.

Against war

Some people refused to join up for the war. They were called conscientious objectors. Most people who objected did so because they thought it was wrong to kill. Others did so because they did not think there was a good enough reason to go to war.

Some people gave conscientious objectors a white feather, a sign of cowardice.

Germany on the move

The German war plan involved first defeating France in the west before turning east against France's ally, Russia. To attack France, Germany needed to move its armies through Belgium. Trains were kept busy, moving armies into position for battle. This was called "mobilization."

The French march

Germany went to war with Russia on August 1, 1914. France and Russia had agreed to help one another. On August 3, Germany declared war on France. The French army began to move trainloads of men and supplies. Many more soldiers marched or traveled on horseback.

The British join up

Britain had promised to help Belgium and France. However, the first British army sent to France was small. There were only 100,000 soldiers. War minister Lord Kitchener called for new armies. Soon, 2.5 million men had volunteered to be "Tommies." "Tommy" was a nickname for a British soldier.

The German army
Germany had about 4 million soldiers, and they were all well-trained. Reserve troops were called up and were soon ready for battle, too. Reserves were part-time and retired soldiers.

French strategy
These French soldiers are marching to war along a dusty road. France was sure that its defensive forts, such as those at the city of Verdun, would stop the Germans from advancing. However, French soldiers' bright uniforms made them easy targets, and their weapons were outdated.

British volunteers
Volunteers were eager to sign up as soldiers. Across Britain, friends wanting to serve together joined a "Pals" battalion—an army unit of about 1,000 men. The soldiers in this photograph are waiting for their train at Waterloo Station, London.

Two Fronts

A front was where the two sides' armies faced each other in battles. At the start of the war in 1914, there were two main fronts: the Western Front and the Eastern Front. German armies won victories in the East, but then both sides became stuck in trench warfare on the Western Front.

Western Front

In the west of Europe, German armies attacked Belgium so that they could advance into France. British armies hurried to Belgium and joined France in the fight against Germany.

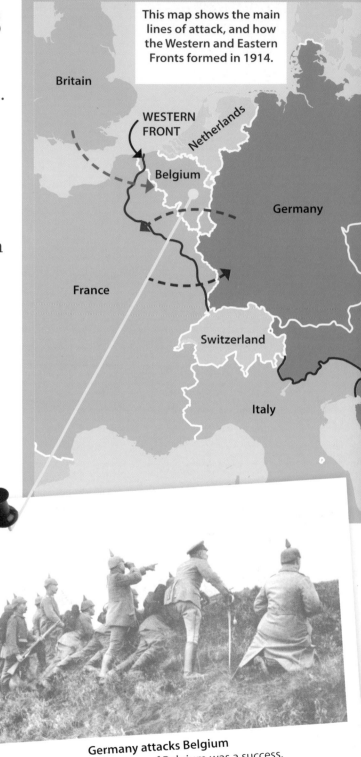

This map shows the main lines of attack, and how the Western and Eastern Fronts formed in 1914.

Britain

WESTERN FRONT

Netherlands

Belgium

Germany

France

Switzerland

Italy

WESTERN FRONT

» **Countries fighting:** Germany, Austria-Hungary, France, Britain, Belgium, Italy

» **Area covered:** less than on the Eastern Front—most fighting was in France and Belgium

» **Movement:** little movement compared to the Eastern Front— armies were bogged down in trenches

» **New weapons:** tanks, aircraft, gas

» **First key battles:** Mons, Belgium and Marne, France (both 1914)

Germany attacks Belgium
The German invasion of Belgium was a success. Within a month, Germany entered France.

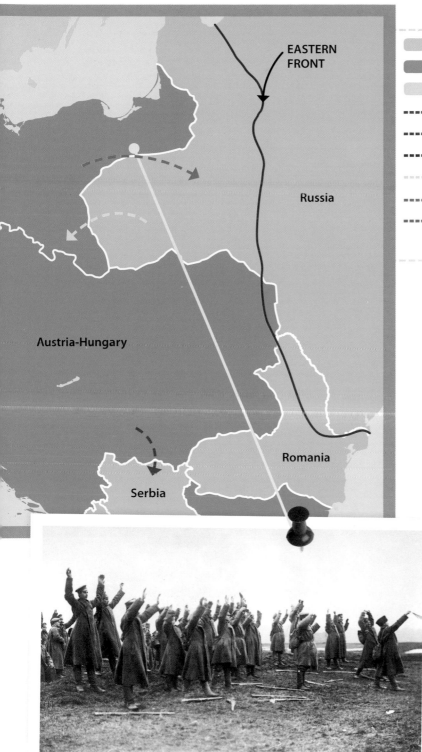

EASTERN FRONT

Russia

Austria-Hungary

Romania

Serbia

KEY

Allies

Central Powers

Neutral (not supporting either side)

---▶ Austria-Hungary attacks Serbia

---▶ Germany advances toward France

---▶ France advances toward Germany

---▶ Russia advances toward Germany

---▶ Germany advances toward Russia

---▶ Britain sends an army to Belgium

Eastern Front

In the east of Europe, Russian armies attacked Germany. Germany struck back. The Russians were badly led, and were defeated. Austria-Hungary attacked Russia and Serbia, but did less well than Germany.

EASTERN FRONT

» **Countries fighting:** Germany, Austria-Hungary, Serbia, Bulgaria, Romania, Turkey, Russia

» **Area covered:** much bigger than the Western Front—included the Baltic countries, such as Serbia, and Russia

» **Movement:** armies marched greater distances than on the Western Front

» **New weapons:** fewer than the Western Front, but did have big artillery guns and field guns

» **First key battles:** Tannenberg and Masurian Lakes (both in Germany, 1914)

Battle of Tannenberg
The Russian army was badly defeated by Germany at the Battle of Tannenberg. Thousands of soldiers were taken prisoner.

War horses

All armies in 1914 had soldiers who rode on horseback. Horses were also used to pull wagons and guns. Horses had some advantages over motor vehicles, which needed roads and often broke down. Horses kept going, even across mountains and deserts where there were no roads. Thousands of horses struggled through the mud of the trench battlefields and some even saved lives.

Cavalry
Soldiers who fought on horseback were called cavalry, like the French cavalrymen shown here. Cavalry moved faster than infantry, who were on foot. They were used as scouts to gather information, and to chase a beaten enemy.

Motor transportation

World War I was the first war in which motor transportation became as important as horses on the battlefield. These women are driving an ambulance through the war zones of France. There was always the chance that a vehicle would break down or get stuck during these early years of motor transportation.

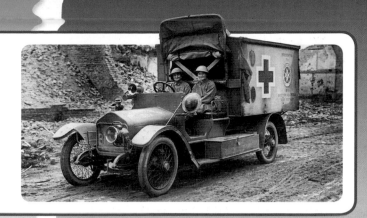

Supply horses

Horses, mules, and donkeys carried supplies to the front. They moved food, water, fuel, tents, and ammunition, including big guns. It was a very dangerous job. Eight million animals were killed doing this vital war work.

Battle horses

Many new soldiers had never ridden a horse. The army taught them to ride, to drive wagons and gun-carriages, and to take care of horses. The first job each morning was to check that the horses were healthy.

Trench warfare

Both sides on the Western Front dug trenches for protection. In these zigzag lines, soldiers faced the enemy, but kept out of sight. Trenches were about 550 yd (500 m) apart. Many were much closer. In between lay an area of land, covered in shell holes. This was "No Man's Land." It was strung with barbed wire higher than a man.

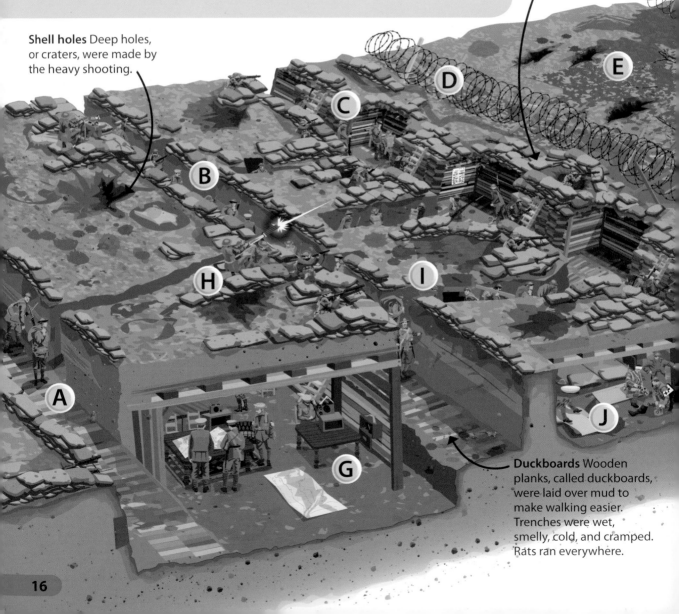

Parapet The front of the trench walls, or parapets, were lined with sandbags filled with soil.

Shell holes Deep holes, or craters, were made by the heavy shooting.

Duckboards Wooden planks, called duckboards, were laid over mud to make walking easier. Trenches were wet, smelly, cold, and cramped. Rats ran everywhere.

Christmas truce

At Christmas 1914, some soldiers stopped fighting for a few hours and held a truce. German and British soldiers left the trenches, shook hands, and exchanged gifts. Some even played soccer. Then the war began again.

Soldiers relaxing at the Christmas truce

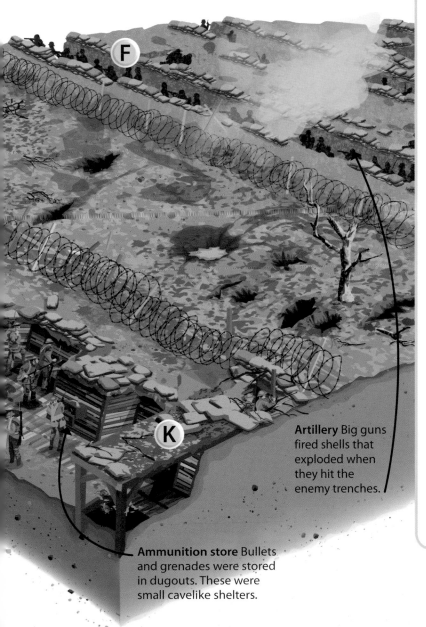

Artillery Big guns fired shells that exploded when they hit the enemy trenches.

Ammunition store Bullets and grenades were stored in dugouts. These were small cavelike shelters.

WHAT'S IN THE PICTURE?

A **Reserve trench** This trench was for fresh troops who were waiting to move up to the front line.

B **Support trench** The second-line trench supported the main trench. Like all trenches, they were at least 6 ft (2 m) deep.

C **Front-line trench** Attacks started from this trench. It was the one closest to the enemy.

D **Barbed wire** This was to stop or slow down enemy soldiers from getting into the opposing trench.

E **No Man's Land** This was the ground between the two opposing trenches. Soldiers crossed it to attack.

F **Enemy trench** Soldiers sometimes saw and heard the enemy in the opposing trench.

G **Command post** Here, officers with maps and telephones planned the next attack.

H **Machine-gun post** Machine guns hidden in "nests" fired across the trenches.

I **Communications trench** This trench linked with others, for men to move from front to rear.

J **Dressing station** A first-aid post for dressing (bandaging) wounds.

K **Listening post** A tunnel where men crawled to spy on the enemy.

A day in the trenches

Between attacks, which were often at daybreak, soldiers spent their time on guard and working. They cleaned their rifles, repaired the trench, ate meals, and whenever the guns were silent, tried to sleep. Many wrote letters or diaries. These are real soldiers' words about their days in the trenches.

Desert to grove

"We have done our best to improve things... We have planted whole bushes of willow and hazel with pretty catkins on them and little firs with their roots, so that a melancholy desert is transformed into an idyllic grove..."
Letter from a German soldier, Lothar Dietz, November 1914

Toiletries

"...I lost all my belongings except the Gillette (razor) so should be glad of a few toilet requisites when next you are sending a parcel. Do not trouble about towel and perhaps Frank would get me a shaving brush. Must now close. Much love to all. From your affectionate son, Dick."
Letter to his mother from Sergeant Dick Gilson, Britain, May 12, 1915

Shaving brush   Button cleaner   Safety razor

Mass of craters

"...the previous night, just in front of our reserve trenches was a beautifully green field, and the next morning it was as much as one could do to see any grass at all, simply one mass of craters..."
Letter from Rifleman Edward Stewart to his friends at work in England, undated

In No Man's Land

"It is a glorious morning and is now broad daylight... we go over in two hours' time. It seems a long time to wait and I think whatever happens, we shall all feel relieved once the line is launched. No Man's Land is a tangled desert..."
Diary of Captain Charlie May, Manchester Regiment Pals Battalion, Britain, written at 5:45 am on the day the Battle of the Somme began, July 1, 1916. He was killed two hours later.

Out in the rain

"One of the worst days of my life. Was out in mud and pouring rain, sopping wet through all day, stretcher-bearing. Returned late at night thoroughly "done in" having lost my way and tumbled into countless trenches, shell holes, etc."
Diary of Lt. Eric Hall, Hampshire Regiment, Britain, October 20, 1916

Stretcher-bearing carrying a stretcher

Cut off for three days

"We had no communication with the rear for three days and nights because the bombardment did not let up. We were not even able to get our rations, and we only ate biscuits and chocolate, and there was almost nothing to drink."
Letter from a French soldier at Verdun, June 1916

Rear support trenches
Bombardment shell fire

Shelling

"They hurl huge shells about a thousand feet into the air and they fall almost vertically. Earth and branches are flung into the air to the height of a house..."
Letter from a German soldier, Karl Josenhans, undated

A heavy shell

Battles at sea

Both Britain and Germany had built up their fleets of battleships (huge warships) ready for war. By 1914 Britain had 29 battleships, and Germany had 18. Submarines proved yet more deadly, sinking many cargo ships.

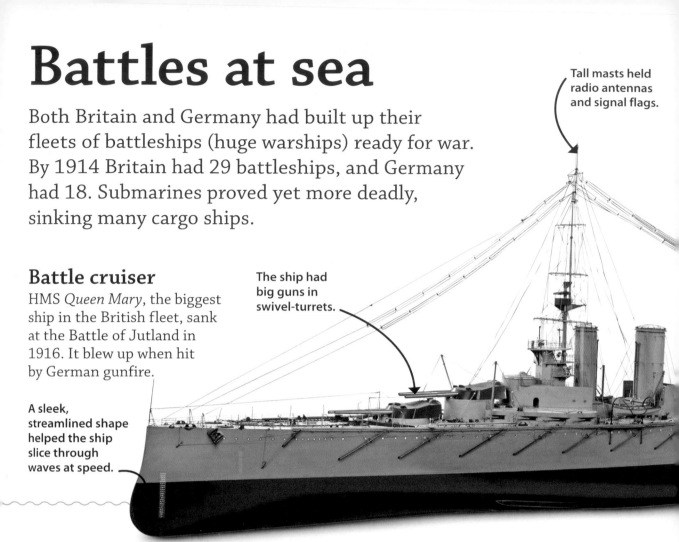

Tall masts held radio antennas and signal flags.

Battle cruiser

HMS *Queen Mary*, the biggest ship in the British fleet, sank at the Battle of Jutland in 1916. It blew up when hit by German gunfire.

The ship had big guns in swivel-turrets.

A sleek, streamlined shape helped the ship slice through waves at speed.

FACT FILE

» **Speed:** 17 knots (19 mph/31 kph)

» **Crew:** 79 men

» **Weapons:** 4 small guns, plus cutting wires to clear enemy mines

Convoy escort

HMS *Snapdragon* was a small British ship. Its job was to sweep (clear) mines and guard supply ships. Sailing in convoys (groups) protected cargo ships from submarines.

Light cruiser

Cruisers were smaller than battleships, but faster for quick attacks. The German cruiser *Regensburg* fought at the biggest sea battle, the Battle of Jutland.

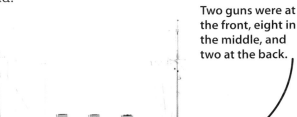

Two guns were at the front, eight in the middle, and two at the back.

Propellers (or "screws") were driven by steam turbine engines.

A U-boat captain looked for enemy ships from the conning tower.

Battle of Jutland

The biggest sea battle was fought between British and German battleships off the coast of Denmark, in the North Sea. Britain lost 14 ships and Germany 11. There was no clear winner, but the German fleet did not risk fighting again.

U-Boat

The U-9 was a German submarine, or "undersea boat." In 1914 it sank three British cruisers in less than an hour. That one attack showed how dangerous submarines could be.

Ships fighting in the North Sea, 1916

Battles in the skies

The first warplanes had no guns. Pilots in 1914 could report what was happening on the ground, but they did not actually fight. This soon changed. Battles in the skies began, and bombs and machine guns were used. Fighter planes got faster, bombers got bigger, and balloons and airships joined the air war.

TRAINING

AVRO 504

The Avro 504 was a biplane, meaning it had two pairs of wings, one above the other, like most aircraft in World War I. For learner pilots, it was an ideal plane to fly—it was simple, strong, and slow, flying at speeds of 90 mph (145 kph). Almost 9,000 Avro 504s were made.

BALLOON

OBSERVATION BALLOON

Balloons were used for getting information. The crewman stood in a basket beneath the balloon and called in reports to the ground, while floating up to 4,000 ft (1,220 m) high. The crewman had a parachute in case the balloon was shot down.

BOMBER

HANDLEY PAGE 0/400

The largest planes were bombers, like this British HP 0/400. This aircraft was 100 ft (30 m) across the wings. It had a crew of five and could fly for eight hours at 97 mph (156 kph). It could carry 2,000 lb (900 kg) of bombs.

FIGHTER

FOKKER DR-1 TRIPLANE

A triplane had three pairs of wings, making it good for twisting and turning in air battles. The Fokker DR-1 fighter was Germany's answer to the Allies' fast Sopwith Triplane. German ace pilot Manfred von Richthofen (the Red Baron) flew a red Fokker Triplane.

AIRSHIP

GERMAN ZEPPELIN

Airships were giant gas-balloons with propellers. Their engines and crew were in cabins, called gondolas, underneath. Some also had gunners. Zeppelin airships flew across the North Sea to bomb Britain. The gas easily caught fire, so airships often burst into flames if hit by bullets.

SCOUT

CAUDRON G-3

Scout planes flew over battlefields to see what the other side was doing. The French Caudron G-3 (1914–1917) had no guns. It had a pilot and an observer, who could take photos. Its top speed was only 67 mph (108 kph).

Aircraft symbol

Each air force marked its planes with its own symbol, called insignia. France used the colors of the French flag. Most insignia were disks, but Germany's was a cross.

Britain

France

Germany

US

Italy

Air aces

At first, World War I pilots were not sent out to fight. Their job was to spot enemy targets. Pilots might even wave if they met an enemy plane. Later, fliers began shooting and dropping bombs. Star fighter pilots were called "aces." To be an ace, a pilot had to score five or more victories in air battles or one-to-one fights, called "dogfights."

Manfred von Richthofen of Germany was the top ace of World War I, with 80 victories. He was known as the Red Baron because he later flew a red plane. He won his first battle on September 17, 1916. This is the story of that fight.

German Albatros planes are patrolling over France. The pilots are watching out for enemy aircraft. Suddenly, they spy British FE2 spotter planes in the distance …

The German planes swoop closer. They start to attack. The planes twist and turn in the sky to avoid being hit.

One plane heads straight toward the Red Baron! The Baron acts fast. He fires his aircraft's machine gun. The British pilot swerves, and his gunner shoots back.

RAT-AT-AT-AT-T!

The Baron's bullets hit the FE2's propeller. Its engine starts to smoke …

SMASH!

The FE2 spirals down and crashes. The Baron has his first victory.

Both British crewmen died in the attack. Later, the Baron visits the pilot's grave to honor him.

The Baron is awarded the Blue Max medal, Germany's highest military honor. In 1918, he himself is killed in action. The legend of the Red Baron lives on—he was a man respected and admired, even by his enemies.

Ace pilots

Most spotter planes had a pilot and a gunner, who also acted as an observer. Fighter pilots flew alone, without even a parachute. Here are three of the most famous ace pilots. Two were killed in action, and only one survived the war.

Albert Ball
British, 44 victories
Killed 1917

Georges Guynemer
French, 54 victories
Killed 1917

William (Billy) Bishop
Canadian, 72 victories
Died 1956

Wartime intelligence

Wartime intelligence is finding out what the enemy is planning and then communicating this back to your own side. At the time of World War I, it was difficult to send messages quickly. There were no cell phones, and radios were too heavy to carry.

Communication

Signals using flags or rockets were often the only way to send a message. Written or coded messages had to be carried, or sent by field telephone or radio.

Dog with a message fixed to its collar

Dog messenger
Dogs were often used to send messages. A dog could run faster than a human, and was nimbler than a horse rider or motor cyclist.

Field telephone
Phone lines to the trenches were buried under the ground. Long stretches of wires linked the field telephones to headquarters.

German radio station on wheels

Radio
Radio messages were sent by tapping them in Morse code. Messages could be sent over very short distances and on land only, but by 1915, some aircraft had radios.

On the lookout

Keeping a lookout on enemy activity, called surveillance, was important. Any new intelligence needed to be sent as quickly as possible to your own side.

Observation equipment
This German officer is using binoculars to see into the distance. His companion has periscope binoculars on a stand, useful when in a trench. He could spot where enemy artillery guns or soldiers were hidden.

French soldier releasing pigeons

Carrier pigeons
Pigeons flew fast and were great for carrying messages. The messages were tied to their legs. Thousands of pigeons went to war, though they did not like flying on wet days.

REALLY?

Buses made great **mobile homes** for **army carrier pigeons**.

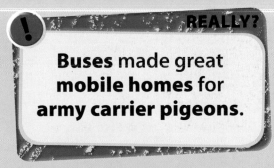

Air photos
Pilots took photos from their aircraft. The photos could be pieced together to show the whole battlefield.

Pilot unloading a camera from a plane

Spying

Both sides used spies to find out what the enemy was doing. Many spies were in the military, such as Carl Lody, a German naval officer, who bravely went into enemy territory. Other spies, such as the Dutch dancer Mata Hari, learned secrets by getting soldiers to talk to her. Spying was dangerous. If a spy was caught, the punishment was death.

Carl Lody spoke English, but had little training as a spy.

Codes and ciphers

A code hides a message by replacing one word with another. A cipher changes each letter for a number or another letter. Armies and secret agents used codes and ciphers for secret messages. Code-breakers tried to "crack" their meaning.

HIDDEN GOODS

Disguise was always useful. This ordinary-looking meat can was a gift for a soldier in a German prison camp. Hidden inside was an escape kit, with maps and wire cutters.

Secret agents

German agent Carl Lody was sent to spy on Britain's navy in 1914. His reports were in code, but were easy to read, so the British secret service soon knew he was a spy. Lody was caught in Ireland. After trial, he was shot in the Tower of London.

Nurse-hero

Edith Cavell was a British nurse in a Red Cross hospital in Belgium. When the Germans came, she was trapped. She continued nursing, and she also helped Allied soldiers escape to neutral (non-fighting) Holland. The Germans shot her like a spy for "helping the enemy."

OBSERVATION POST

Soldiers spied on the enemy from all kinds of observation posts. They kept watch from trenches, buildings, hilltops, and tall trees. When real trees had been flattened by gunfire, a dummy tree made from metal made a good watchtower.

Trench periscope

Putting your head above a trench was dangerous, with enemy sharpshooters on watch. Using a trench periscope was safer. These German officers are using one here. They were at the front in 1916.

Invisible ink

1 2
3 4

Invisible ink is made from chemicals, or even milk or lemon juice. Dip a pen in juice, write on paper, and nothing can be seen. Warm the paper, and writing appears! Most spies used chemical ink.

Great coat for warmth

Britain
British troops had swapped red coats for khaki brown in the late 1800s. Pilots needed thick coats, with gloves and boots to keep warm.

Goggles

Helmet

Notebook

Sheepskin hat

Russia
Russian soldiers were not as well equipped as others. Many wore soft hats for warmth, but they did not protect their heads as well as metal helmets. But at least their gear was light to carry.

France
At the start of the war, French soldiers wore bright blue tunics and red pants. But these made them too easy to spot. By 1915, French soldiers wore blue-gray.

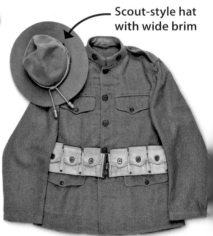

Scout-style hat with wide brim

Uniforms

By the time of World War I, uniforms started to change. In the past, soldiers could easily tell friend from enemy by their uniform. By 1918, most soldiers looked much the same. Gone were the old bright, shiny uniforms. In came duller shades of browns and grays, which were harder for the enemy to pick out.

United States
US soldiers wore tunics like European soldiers. Belts and pouches were packed with bullets and their kit. Many soldiers carried a weight of about 60 lb (27 kg)!

Identity tags showed each soldier's name and army number

Austria-Hungary

Austria-Hungary's army had modern uniforms like those of German soldiers. However, these men on parade still carried swords.

Germany

German uniform was a special gray, called "field-gray." The old spiked leather helmet was replaced with a metal helmet. Some soldiers still had a sword as well as a gun.

New helmet

Old helmet

13

Thick coat

Sword

Leather boots

Soft hat

Shoulder loop, or epaulet

Ottoman Empire

Turkish soldiers wore brown uniforms and hats. These soldiers have cloth strips, or puttees, wound around their legs. British soldiers wore puttees, too.

Medals

To show a soldier's rank, stripes, stars, or crowns were sewn on the uniform's sleeve or shoulder. Medals for bravery were normally worn only on special occasions. Here are three wartime medals, or decorations.

Military Cross, Britain

Iron Cross, Germany

Order of Osmanieh, Turkey

Gas warfare

Poison gas was a deadly chemical weapon. It could blind a soldier, damage skin and lungs, and leave him feeling sick. Troops wore gas masks to protect themselves. The Germans used gas first, in April 1915. Later, both sides used gas.

Gas masks for all
These German soldiers are wearing gas masks to protect their eyes and throats. Their donkey has a mask too, with a strap to hold it on.

Chemical war

By 1915, factory workers were making gases to be used in warfare. Some people thought that gas was less cruel than bullets. Gas did not usually kill soldiers—it just put them out of action.

French soldiers checking gas cylinders

Gas cylinders
In 1915, armies released gas from metal cylinders or cans. The gas cloud blew across the battlefield toward the enemy trenches. Sometimes the wind changed, and the gas swirled back.

French police on bikes ready for a gas attack

Gas mask patrols
Sometimes towns and cities close to battlefields were in danger from gas attacks, too. These French police are wearing gas masks to protect themselves on patrol.

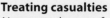

German nurses treating gas casualties

Treating casualties
Nurses took care of victims of gas attacks at casualty stations and hospitals. Some soldiers had to be sent home, but others were passed fit to fight again in the next battle.

Gallipoli

The Gallipoli battle of 1915 was a plan that went wrong. The Allies decided to land troops in Gallipoli in Turkey, to knock Turkey out of the war, and help Russia. The attack was meant to capture an important sea route, the Dardanelles. The plan failed. After months of fighting and losses, the Allies withdrew.

The battle
The Gallipoli land battle began on April 25, after a failed Allied sea attack. The Allies landed 75,000 soldiers, but found 60,000 Turkish soldiers ready for them. Fighting was fierce. Losses on both sides were huge. By the end, there were over 500,000 soldiers killed, wounded, or missing.

ANZACs

Thousands of troops from Australia and New Zealand came to fight alongside Britain. They joined the Australian and New Zealand Army Corps, and so became known as "ANZACs." About half the soldiers who first landed at Gallipoli were ANZACs.

Beach landings
Allied soldiers traveled over in ships, and then were taken by small boats to the Turkish beaches. The Turkish soldiers had strong defenses, and their gunfire stopped the Allies from moving far inland.

Sea channel

Gallipoli is a strip of land beside a narrow sea channel, called the Dardanelles. The waterway was important because it gave Russian ships a route from the Black Sea into the Mediterranean Sea.

The Gallipoli war zone

Slouch hat

Many Australians and New Zealanders wore wide-brimmed slouch hats as part of their uniform. The hat became a symbol of ANZAC bravery. It is shown here with a Remembrance poppy.

"The Australian and New Zealand troops have indeed proved themselves worthy sons of the Empire."
GEORGE R.I.

Honoring the ANZACs

This poster honors the ANZACs who fought at Gallipoli. It has a message from Britain's King George V on it.

Women in wartime

While men were away fighting, women took on jobs previously done by men. Women worked in factories, offices, on farms, and in transportation. Others trained as nurses, and risked their lives in war zones. This was a huge change for women. Before the war, many women had not worked outside the home.

Farm workers

Farms needed people to plant and harvest crops, to plow and drive carts. These women are busy working in a field on a French farm.

Office workers

Many women went out to work for the first time. Some found office jobs as typists and clerks, dealing with wartime paperwork. These women are updating identification papers.

Factory workers

Factories needed workers to make weapons, uniforms, and vehicles. Women used factory machines like this one to make hand grenades for the army.

Nurses

Most war nurses were women. Some left home for the first time to work in hospitals. Others went to nurse sick and wounded soldiers on the battlefields.

Ambulance drivers

More women learned to drive. Some women drove ambulances, such as these in France. They moved wounded men from the trenches to hospitals in safe areas.

Bus conductors

At home, some women took jobs as bus conductors. Many buses had open tops, so the conductor needed a coat and boots, as well as a money bag and ticket machine.

Desert fighting

British soldiers and their allies fought battles in the hot, dry deserts of the Middle East. Here, they defeated the army of the Ottoman Empire. Arab peoples rebelled against Turkish rule. They were helped by British soldiers, including T.E. Lawrence, later known as Lawrence of Arabia.

Sand shoes were worn over boots to help stop soldiers from sinking into soft sand.

These Arab soldiers are crossing hot desert lands. Camel troops could travel 40 miles (64 km) a day.

Jerusalem

Jerusalem in the Middle East is a holy city to Christians, Jews, and Muslims. At the beginning of World War I, it was under the rule of the Ottoman Empire. In 1917, it was captured by British and Arab armies. The British General Allenby led his troops into the ancient city on foot, as a mark of respect.

General Allenby entering Jerusalem in 1917

Mountain fighting

Some of the hardest fighting took place high in Europe's mountain range—the Alps. Here, Italian and Austrian soldiers fought battles over peaks and passes.

Mountain troops needed to be comfortable with heights.

Mountain climbing

Specially trained soldiers, or alpine troops, climbed steep, slippery rocks to get above the enemy. Even in winter snow and ice, they dragged guns up mountains. Mules carried their supplies along narrow tracks.

Boots

Alpine soldiers wore thick climbing boots to protect their feet and support their ankles when climbing.

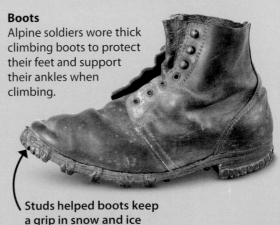

Studs helped boots keep a grip in snow and ice

REALLY?

A camel could carry the **weight of** about **3 men.**

Two great battles

In 1916, two of the biggest battles of the war were fought in France. First, Germany attacked Verdun, a city with army forts that lay close to the German border. Later, in July, a battle along the Somme River began. This attack was planned by the Allies to help France, which was losing the battle at Verdun. These two battles raged for almost a year. More than 1.5 million soldiers were killed or wounded.

February 21, 1916
About 1,400 large weapons (artillery) are fired at the start of the attack on Verdun. The gunfire lasts over seven hours.

German infantry (foot) soldier

June 7, 1916
Germany captures Fort Vaux, and then moves troops to the Eastern Front to fight a Russian attack.

German soldiers in a trench

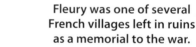
Fleury was one of several French villages left in ruins as a memorial to the war.

July 1, 1916
Britain attacks on the Somme River. There are 19,000 soldiers killed on the first day. France joins the battle.

August 18, 1916
The Battle of Verdun still rages. France recaptures Fleury village. The Germans weaken.

Hardships of war

The British and French attacked along the Somme River while the battle for Verdun was still being fought. In battles of tanks, mines, and mud, thousands died and little ground was won.

Tanks
Tanks were a new surprise weapon in the war. This British tank is crossing a trench as soldiers use it for cover.

German field gun, a typical artillery weapon

February 25, 1916
Specially trained German "stormtroopers" use flame-thrower weapons and grenades as they capture Fort Douaumont, the highest fort at Verdun.

Fort Douaumont at Verdun

May 6, 1916
A new railroad and thousands of trucks bring supplies. France holds Verdun, though Germany captures key hills.

General Pétain of France

March 6, 1916
Army general Philippe Pétain orders French troops to defend the inner forts at Verdun at all costs.

October 24, 1916
Despite bad weather, France takes back Fort Douamont, and then Vaux a month later.

French soldiers firing grenades

December 17, 1916
Germany stops attacking. The French still hold Verdun. About 900,000 have been killed or wounded in the battles.

Mines
Mines were set off to explode under German defenses at the Somme, and here on Messines Ridge in Belgium. The explosions could be heard in England.

Mud
Mud was the soldier's enemy too, in the trenches on the Somme, and here at Passchendaele, France, in 1917.

WOW!

Tank tracks soon wore out. They had to be changed about every **20 miles (32 km)**.

Armor

Metal armor protected the men inside, but made the vehicle heavy. This tank weighed about 28 tons (25 tonnes).

The British Mark V tank was first used in 1918, the final year of the war. It played an important part in Allied advances.

919

Tanks at war

Tanks were a British invention, and were used for the first time in 1916. These crawling metal monsters had tracks that helped them cross trenches and smash through wire. Tanks were best used in large numbers, like cavalry troops.

Gun crew

Gunners fired two big guns. There were also three quick-firing machine guns. Eight men sat squeezed inside the hot and stuffy tank.

Driver

The driver peered through a slit with a flap. Steering was tricky. It was like driving a tractor. Two other crewmen used gear levers to turn the tank.

Into battle

British tanks first went into battle on September 15, 1916 in the Battle of the Somme, in France. Thirty-six tanks started, but most got stuck or broke down. Later in the war, tanks became more reliable.

Early 1916 tank with rear steering wheels

Commander

The commander was in charge. He directed where the tank was to go and gave orders. He sat next to the driver and worked the brake.

Ammunition

Shells were stacked beside the two guns. Each shell weighed 6 lb (2.7 kg). The guns were loaded by hand.

Caterpillar tracks

The idea for tank tracks came from farm tractors. The track was a loop of metal plates. On tracks, a tank could crawl over ditches and even walls.

The US at war

At first, the US wanted no part in World War I. However, US factories were busy making war weapons for Britain and France. Three important events helped push the US to war in 1917, when President Wilson declared war on Germany.

1915

1916

Lusitania sunk

The German submarine U-20 sank the British passenger ship *Lusitania* crossing the ocean to the US. More than 1,000 passengers drowned. The sinking turned many in the US against Germany.

A lifebelt from RMS *Lusitania*. The ship was sunk without warning.

Black Tom explosions

Explosions shook New York City in the US. Fire on a pier called Black Tom set off explosives. The huge blast damaged the torch on the Statue of Liberty (above). The US blamed this attack on German agents.

> **!** In 1917, Germany promised to help **Mexico** get back the state of **Texas** from the **US**.

The US in Europe

The US sent men, weapons, and money to help the Allies. Factories worked to produce more weapons, and people at home were encouraged to help the war effort.

Recruitment poster
Posters urged men to join the army. In 1914 the US Army had 128,000 soldiers. By 1918 it had 4 million. After a few weeks' training, soldiers left by ship for Europe.

Posters called on people's patriotism (love of country).

1917

Soldier writing a letter home

To the Front
The arrival of US armies helped the Allies. US soldiers learned about trench war, but many missed home.

Zimmerman telegram

The coded telegram

Germany hoped Mexico might fight against the US. German government minister Alfred Zimmerman (above) sent the Mexicans a telegram in code promising German help. British agents read it, and told the US.

War heroes
US soldiers fought bravely and some were honored as war heroes. These included pilot Eddie Rickenbacker and soldier Alvin York, who were awarded the Distinguished Service Cross for bravery.

Distinguished Service Cross (US)

Russian Revolution

By 1917 Russia's people were sick of war. Huge numbers of soldiers had been killed and many people at home were starving and living in poverty. They blamed their ruler, Tsar Nicholas II. In March, the people rebelled and the tsar gave up his throne. In October, the Bolsheviks (Communists) seized power.

Russian battleship *Potem*

The tsar with his family

The tsar and his family

Tsar Nicholas II lived a life of luxury and had lost touch with the plight of his people. After the tsar gave up the throne, he and his family were arrested and later executed by the Bolsheviks (Communists) in July 1918.

Lenin takes control

Lenin was the leader of the Bolshevik (Communist) Party. He rallied people together and promised an end to the war and to food shortages. After the October Revolution, Russia became a Communist country called the Soviet Union. Lenin was its new leader.

Mutiny on a ship

Revolution was not new in Russia. In 1905, sailors on the battleship *Potemkin* suffered poor working conditions. They rebelled and joined city workers on strike. This rebellion, or mutiny, failed, but it encouraged others to revolution.

The Communist red flag showed a hammer and sickle, representing factory and farm workers.

Cossacks

Russian soldiers fought bravely in the war. They included the Cossacks, who were feared cavalry fighters. They fought on horseback with swords and spears. Many Cossacks hated the Bolsheviks, and fought against the revolution.

Russia and Germany agree peace terms in March 1918

No more war?

Germany welcomed the October Revolution, as it led to a ceasefire between Germany and Russia, and an end to the war on the Eastern Front. Germany could now focus on the Western Front.

War propaganda

Propaganda is using words and pictures to influence people in the way they think. Governments on both sides used war propaganda to show their country as good and brave, and the enemy as bad and cowardly. Sometimes, lies were told, too. Books, newspapers, movies, and posters were all used as part of the propaganda war.

Joining up

In 1914 most people felt a love of their country. They cheered men joining the army, hoping the war would soon be over. But that hope died. By 1917 posters were still calling on people to fight.

Recruitment poster, US

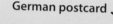
German postcard

Signing up for the army in France

Follow the flag

Patriotic postcards sold well. This one has the words "I am a German" above a picture of a German soldier wearing a helmet and proudly carrying his country's flag.

War movies

World War I took place during the early years of film. War movies were shot in black and white, and were silent. Battle scenes were often filmed during training because real battlefields were too dangerous for camera crews.

Filming with the army of Austria-Hungary

British poster asking people not to waste food from overseas

DO YOUR BIT

H.M.S.

SAVE·FOOD

Selling "Liberty Bonds" in the US

War bonds

Wars cost a lot of money. So governments asked people to lend their savings by buying "war bonds." In the US, these were called "Liberty Bonds."

Posters

Posters had pictures and messages to aid the war effort. Some Allied posters were anti-German. Others asked people to work hard, save food, and help win the war.

Recording the war

What we know about the war comes from people who lived through it. Writers and artists, photographers and journalists, songwriters, and ordinary men and women recorded what happened. They tell us what it was like to be in the thick of war.

Paintings

In 1916, Britain's first official war artists went to paint the battlefields of France. Painters showed what war was really like. They did not glorify it, like some magazine illustrations did. This painting by John Nash shows soldiers in battle at Ypres in Belgium.

NEWSPAPERS

People got war news from newspapers. They had no radio at home, no television, and no Internet. This 1914 German newspaper is reporting a German victory—the capture of the city of Liège in Belgium. Governments put news of victories in the headlines, but often hid stories of defeats.

SONGS

Soldiers and people at home sang and whistled popular songs. They bought printed sheet music to play and sing at home. *Over There* was a hit song about the arrival of American troops, who began traveling to Europe in 1917.

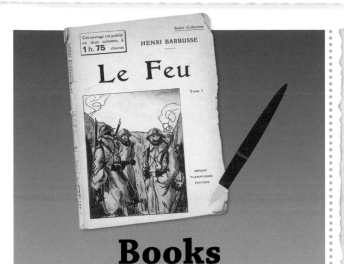

Books

Many novels were written about the war. One of the best is *Le Feu* (*Under Fire*, 1916) by French writer Henri Barbusse. He came to hate all war after being wounded while fighting on the Western Front.

Poems

War poets wrote about the horrors of battle, but at times they found moments of hope and calm too, in a flower or a bird's song. British soldier Wilfred Owen wrote moving war poems. Tragically, he was killed a week before fighting stopped in 1918.

Wilfred Owen

LETTERS

Soldiers wrote home to their loved ones. Families and friends wrote back. These letters tell us how people felt and how they got on with their lives as best they could. Some soldiers wrote diaries. These, too, are a priceless record of people at war.

Movies

Movies could be used to lift people's spirits. Movie star Charlie Chaplin appeared in many silent comic movies. In his comedy *Shoulder Arms* (1918) he plays a soldier in France, who captures 13 Germans and Kaiser Wilhelm II. It turns out to be just a dream.

The last battles

In 1918, Germany made a last effort to win on the Western Front. Its armies gathered 6,000 huge artillery guns for a big attack, but the Allies drove the Germans back. Germany was exhausted, and by October 1918 knew the war was lost. The Kaiser gave up his throne, and Germany asked for an armistice (ceasefire).

Amiens breakthrough

By August 1918, the Allies had more tanks, more planes, and fresh troops from the US. They won the Battle of Amiens, in France, and the Germans began to retreat (move back). For the next 100 days, the Allies were on the attack toward Germany's last defenses.

Fighting in ruined buildings

Battle of the Marne

German armies attacked on March 21, 1918, in fog. For a time, the Allies struggled. Then, British, French, Canadian, and Australian troops stopped the Germans at the second Battle of the Marne. The Marne River in France was where battles began in 1914. The war was back where it started.

Gun crews get ready

Allied troops by the canal

The Hindenburg Line

The last German defense was called the Hindenburg Line, named after top German general, Paul von Hindenburg. The Allies attacked through the Argonne Forest and captured the St. Quentin Canal. By October 1918, German defenses had been broken.

US armies

The US armies in France were led by General Pershing. The US brought new energy to the Allies and fresh hope to the battles.

US soldiers on the march

American might

The US had factories and money, as well as soldiers. The strength and wealth of the US gave the Allies the advantage. US money and power helped the Allies, and made President Wilson an important world leader.

Peace

US President Wilson put forward a 14-point peace plan. Germany agreed. With its soldiers beaten and its economy in ruins, it had no choice. German leaders asked for an armistice, or final ceasefire. At 11 am on November 11, 1918, the fighting stopped.

US newspaper announcing the end of the war

Armistice
On November 11, 1918, an armistice (ceasefire) was declared. It brought rejoicing to the Allies—they had won, and the Central Powers had lost. Here, crowds in the US are celebrating victory and their troops' homecoming.

Peace at last

After peace was declared, people celebrated. But while millions of soldiers returned home, there was sadness, too. More than 65 million men had gone to war. About half were now dead, wounded, missing, or prisoners. Many soldiers who had survived tried to forget what they had seen on the battlefields.

Troops head home
A million Americans had gone to war in France. Now they came home by ship, like these men in December 1918. The war took many soldiers overseas for the first time.

Treaty signed
In June 1919, leaders from the nations at war met at Versailles in France. They signed a treaty (agreement) settling the peace terms to end "the war to end wars."

Remembering the war

After the war, people knew they must never forget. On the battlefields, war cemeteries were laid out with the graves of those killed. Many had no known graves. Injured soldiers who came home needed help, too. To this day, ceremonies are held to remember those who suffered and died.

German war memorial
War memorials, like this one in Munich, Germany, remind us of those who went to war. Some memorials bear many names, including those from the same families.

Laid to rest
This is the war cemetery at Vis-en-Artois, at Arras in France. War graves are laid out in long rows on the land where soldiers died. Here people visit to remember those who died.

Heroes remembered

This US monument stands in New York City. It honors soldiers of the 307th Infantry Regiment, which fought in France in 1918. Like many other war statues, it shows soldiers in action.

The poppy has been a symbol of remembrance of war since 1921. Its use was inspired by a war poem about poppy flowers covering battlefields.

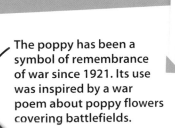

Remembrance poppy

In 2014, the Tower of London in England was used to mark 100 years since World War I began. People placed thousands of ceramic poppies around the tower walls. Each poppy represented a soldier killed in the war.

World War I facts and figures

World War I was also called the Great War. Here are some facts about the biggest war that the world had ever seen.

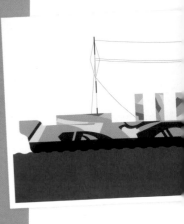

FIVE CARIBOU MEMORIALS were set up in France and Belgium for soldiers from Newfoundland in Canada who died in World War I.

Fastest tank: **Whippet** (9 mph/14 kph)

16 YEARS

was the age of British boy-sailor Jack Cornwell when he was fatally wounded at the Battle of Jutland in 1916.

33,000

camels were used by the Allies in desert warfare.

Some supply ships were painted in **"DAZZLE CAMOUFLAGE."** Its crazy patterns and colors helped disguise the ship's shape, confusing the enemy.

Top secret weapons

Tanks were first called "landships.x" The British gave them the code-name "**tanks**" to pretend they were for water storage, and not secret new weapons.

Who had the BIGGEST ARMY?

Russia—**12 million**

Germany—nearly **11 million**

Britain and France—about **8 million** each

US—**4 million**

1 soldier represents 1 million soldiers

The Spanish flu outbreak at the end of the war killed more people than the war itself. Between **50–100 million** people died, and one in three of the world's population fell sick.

16,000

was the approximate number of British men who refused to fight, because of anti-war beliefs.

More than

500,000

pigeons carried messages between headquarters and the front lines.

Glossary

Some words in this book may be new to you. This is what they mean. They will help you to learn about World War I.

air raid Attack from the sky by aircraft dropping bombs

airship Balloonlike floating aircraft filled with gas, but with engines and propellers

Allies Countries and peoples working together toward a shared aim

armistice Agreement between armies to stop fighting and start peace talks

assassination Killing someone, often a leader, for a political reason

barbed wire Coils of wire with twists and points (barbs); it was used in trench defenses

battleship Large warship with thick metal armor and big guns

bayonet Long swordlike weapon that fits to a soldier's rifle

Bolshevik Member of a communist revolutionary group in Russia

casualty Someone killed or wounded in battle

cavalry Group of soldiers who ride horses

civil war Fighting between opposing groups of people in the same country

code Way to keep a message secret by changing what it says. Knowing the code means someone can read it

communism Way of life in which everything belongs to the state, or government

convoy Group of ships sailing together, with warships to guard them

field telephone Communications system using telephones linked by long wires between trenches and command posts

fighter plane Fast plane with guns, used to fight and shoot down enemy planes

fleet Large group of ships

gas mask Gogglelike mask worn over the nose and mouth to stop people from breathing in poison gas

grenade Small bomb thrown by a soldier

headquarters (HQ) Place where commanders worked and sent out orders to their armies

British women ambulance drivers

helmet Metal hat to protect a soldier's head from flying shell fragments, stones, and even bullets. Armies began the war with soft hats, but soon changed to helmets

incendiary Able to catch fire. In the war, incendiary fire-bullets and fire-bombs were used

infantry Soldiers who normally fight on foot; most of the trench soldiers were infantry

machine gun Rapid-firing gun, usually needing a team of three or four men to carry, load, and fire it; it could fire up to 600 bullets a minute

mobilization Preparing for war by moving armies into position for battle

Morse code Code using dots and dashes for letters. Morse code can be sent by flashing lights, by sounds (taps), or by electrical signals

neutral Not taking part in a war. Belgium was a neutral country until attacked by Germany. Switzerland, Sweden, and Spain were neutral all through the war

Remembrance Day poppy

observer Someone who is on the lookout. In a two-man aircraft, the observer looked for signs of the enemy, reported movements, and also fired the plane's machine gun in air battles

offensive Army name for a very big attack, often using thousands of soldiers

periscope Tube with mirrors for seeing without being seen yourself, used by submarines and in trenches

poison gas Chemical weapons, such as mustard gas, used against soldiers. Poison gas can kill or hurt people so badly they are unable to fight

propeller Spinning blades on an aircraft engine that drive the plane

puttees Strips of cloth wound around a soldier's pants from below the knee to his boots. Puttees kept the pants dry, and gave extra protection against stones and dust

ration Soldier's food supply. Rationing means fixing the amount of food for each person, to share supplies fairly

revolution Movement or uprising against a government by people wanting to set up a new kind of government

rifle Long handgun usually fired from a standing position or lying flat

scout Soldier or aircraft sent to see where the enemy is

spy Person who gathers information in secret. In war, each side uses spies to find the other's secrets

submarine Boat that can travel under water as well as on the ocean

torpedo Weapon fired from a submarine to travel under water, hit a target ship, and explode, to sink it.

trench Hole or ditch dug in the ground to protect soldiers from gunfire. Trenches zigzagged, and were held up by sandbags, wood, and metal sheets

troops Groups of soldiers

Index

A

aerial photography 27
air aces 24–25
aircraft 22–23
airships 23
Allenby, General 38
Allies 5, 9, 45, 54
Alps 39
ambulance drivers 37
Amiens, Battle of 52
ammunition 17, 43
ANZACs 34–35
Arabs 38–39
armies, size of 59
armistice 53, 54–55
arms race 5
artillery 17
Australia 34–35, 55
Austria-Hungary 4, 6, 8, 13, 31, 39

B

Balkan wars 4
Ball, Albert 25
barbed wire 16, 17
Barbusse, Henri 51
battle horses 15
battleships 20–21
Belgium 7, 12
biplanes 22
Bishop, William (Billy) 25
Black Tom explosions 44
Bolsheviks 46, 47
bombers 22
books 51
Bosnia 6
boys in war 10, 58
Britain 5, 7, 9, 10–11, 30, 59

British Empire 5
Bulgaria 4, 8
bus conductors 37

C

camels 38–39, 58
camouflage 59
Canada 58
carrier pigeons 27, 59
casualties 35, 54
caterpillar tracks 43
cavalry 14
Cavell, Edith 29
cemeteries 56
Central Powers 4, 8, 54
Chaplin, Charlie 51
chemical war 35
Christmas truce (1914) 17
Clemenceau, Georges 9
codes and ciphers 28
communications 26–27
communism 46–47
conscientious objectors 10, 59
convoys 20
Cossacks 47
cruisers 20, 21

D

Dardanelles 34, 35
desert fighting 38–39
diaries 18, 19
disguises 28
dog messengers 26
dogfights 24
duckboards 16

E

Eastern Front 12, 13, 40, 47

F

factory work 36
farm work 36
field telephones 26–27
fighter planes 23
films 47, 48, 51
fleets 20–21
food 15, 19, 39, 46, 49
Fort Douaumont 41
France 5, 7, 9, 10–11, 30, 59
Franz Ferdinand, Archduke 6
Franz Joseph I, Emperor 8

G

Gallipoli, Battle of 34–35
gas 34–35
gas masks 34–35
George V, King 5, 35
Germany 4, 7, 8, 10–11, 31, 45, 47, 52–53, 59
graves 56
Greece 4
grenades 41
Guynemer, Georges 25

H

Hindenburg, General Paul von 53
Hindenburg Line 53
horses 14–15

I

identity tags 31
infantry 14, 57
insignia, air forces 23
intelligence 26–27
invisible ink 29
Italy 9, 3

Acknowledgments

DORLING KINDERSLEY would like to thank: Brenda Williams (text consultant), Polly Goodman for proofreading, and Helen Peters for the index. The publishers would also like to thank the following for their kind permission to reproduce the extracts from the letters and diaries on pp 18–19: Letter from Thomas Harold Watts, http://www.nationalarchives.gov.uk/education/resources/letters-first-world-war-1915/; Letter from Edward Henry Cecil Stewart, http://www.nationalarchives.gov.uk/education/resources/letters-first-world-war-1915/trenches-swept-continually-shells/; Letter by a French soldier in the line before Fleury, http://www.worldwar1.com/tgws/rel012.htm; O'Brien Browne for translation from the original French of Letter from a French soldier at Verdun, 1916; Letter from Lothar Dietz, https://www.theguardian.com/world/2008/nov/10/first-world-war-trenches-life-german, P. Witkop (ed) *German Students' War Letters*, London, 1929, pp 39–43; A Saunders, *Weapons of the Trench War*, Stroud 1999, pp 28–51; cited on p 106 of *Trench*, by Stephen Bull (Osprey 2010); Letter from Karl Josenhans, P. Witkop (ed) *German Students' War Letters*, London, 1929, pp 39–43; A Saunders, *Weapons of the Trench War*, Stroud 1999, pp 28–51; cited on p 106 of *Trench*, by Stephen Bull (Osprey 2010); Letter from Sergeant Dick Gilson; http://www.nationalarchives.gov.uk/education/resources/letters-first-world-war-1915/trenches-mostly-mere-boys/; Diary of Lt Eric Hall, Hampshire Regiment, https://collection.nam.ac.uk/detail.php?acc=2000-01-32-1; Captain Charlie May, quoted in Gerry Harrison (ed) *To Fight Alongside Friends*, p 213, (William Collins 2014).

The publisher would like to thank the following for their kind permission to reproduce their photographs:

(Key: a-above; b-below/bottom; c-centre; f-far; l-left; r-right; t-top)

1 123RF.com: Scott Fensome / zollster (c). 2 Alamy Stock Photo: World History Archive (cb). Depositphotos Inc: fotoatelie (br). Dorling Kindersley: Collection of Jean-Pierre Verney (bc). 3 Alamy Stock Photo: Everett Collection Historical (bc). Dorling Kindersley: Collection of Jean-Pierre Verney (crb); Paul Ford (tr); Royal Green Jackets Museum, Winchester (clb); The Tank Museum (cb). 4 Getty Images: PhotoQuest (r); Topical Press Agency (cb). 5 Alamy Stock Photo: Photo 12 (l) Getty Images: Hulton Archive (bc); SeM (crb). 6 Alamy Stock Photo: World History Archive (tl). Mary Evans Picture Library: Sueddeutsche Zeitung Photo (cr). 7 Alamy Stock Photo: INTERFOTO (tl). Getty Images: DEA/G. DAGLI ORTI (cr); ND (cb). 8 Alamy Stock Photo: GL Archive (clb); World History Archive (cra); World History Archive (crb). 9 Library of Congress, Washington, D.C.: (cla). 10 123RF.com: Andreas Neef (clb). 11 Alamy Stock Photo: Chronicle (t); Glasshouse Images (c); Chronicle (b). 12 Getty Images: SeM (crb). 13 Getty Images: Paul Thompson/FPG (bc). 14 Alamy Stock Photo: Peter Stone-Archive. 15 Alamy Stock Photo: KGPA Ltd (bl). Getty Images: IWM (tr); Popperfoto (br). 17 Alamy Stock Photo: Chronicle (tc). 18–19 123RF.com: pretoperola. 18 Alamy Stock Photo: Everett Collection Historical (br); RedDaxLumav (fcr). Dorling Kindersley: Birmingham Pals (crb). Dreamstime.com: Martina Meyer/Martinam (bc); Suljo (cl). 19 Alamy Stock Photo: Chronicle (br); World History Archive (tr). Dreamstime.com: Carolyn Franks/Whitestar1955 (cr); Jakub Krechowicz Sqback (t). 120–21 National Maritime Museum, Greenwich, London: (c). 20 National Maritime Museum, Greenwich, London. 21 Alamy Stock Photo: INTERFOTO (br). National Maritime Museum, Greenwich, London. SD Model Makers: (cb). 22 Alamy Stock Photo: PF-(sdasm3) (crb); SOTK2011 (clb). Dorling Kindersley: Royal Airforce Museum, London (Hendon) (tr). 22–23 123RF.com: Dmitry Kalinovsky/kadmy (background). 23 Dorling Kindersley: Paul Ford (ca); Royal Airforce Museum, London (cb). Getty Images: Ullstein Bild (cra). 25 Alamy Stock Photo: Classic Image (bc/George); World History Archive (bc); WorldPhotos (br). 26 Alamy Stock Photo: American Photo Archive (r); Universal Images Group North America LLC (clb) Getty Images: IWM (cl). 27 Getty Images: Boyer (crb); Popperfoto (l); Universal History Archive (cra). 28 Getty Images: Popperfoto (bl). 29 Getty Images: adoc-photos (br); Print Collector (cl); Photo 12 (tr). 30 Dorling Kindersley: (tl) (crb). 31 Alamy Stock Photo: World History Archive (bc) Dorling Kindersley. Getty Images: FPG (cr); Imagno (cl) 32–33 Alamy Stock Photo: World History Archive. 33 Alamy Stock Photo: PRISMA ARCHIVO (c); The Print Collector (ca); Trinity Mirror/Mirrorpix (cb). 34–35 Alamy Stock Photo: Chronicle (t). 34 Alamy Stock Photo: Granger Historical Picture Archive (crb). 35 Alamy Stock Photo: Lordprice Collection (bc); Photography (clb). 36 Alamy Stock Photo: Everett Collection Historical (cr); Photo 12 (tr). Getty Images: Jacques Boyer/Roger Viollet (bl) 37 Alamy Stock Photo: GL Archive (tl); Science History Images (clb); Lebrecht Music and Arts Photo Library (cr) 38–39 Alamy Stock Photo: Chronicle. Dorling Kindersley. 38 Getty Images: Photo 12 (cr). 39 Alamy Stock Photo: Everett Collection Historical (cra). Getty Images: DEA/G. CIGOLINI (crb). 40 Alamy Stock Photo: KGPA Ltd (cr); Prisma by Dukas Presseagentur GmbH (crb); Lordprice Collection (cr). Depositphotos Inc: fotoatelie (cra). 41 Alamy Stock Photo: akg-images (cra); Lebrecht Music and Arts Photo Library (cb); Photo 12 (clb); Granger Historical Picture Archive (cl). Dorling Kindersley: Royal Museum of the Armed Forces and of Military History, Brussels, Belgium (tl). Getty Images: Topical Press Agency (ca). 43 Bovington Tank Museum: (cra). 44 Getty Images: Interim Archives (cl). 45 Getty Images: Bettmann (cr); Paul Popper Popperfoto (cl); David Pollack (cra); Bettmann (br). 46 123RF.com: aomarch (background). Alamy Stock Photo: IanDagnall Computing (cl). Getty Images: Hulton Archive (cra). 46–47 123RF.com: Maksim Kostenko. Alamy Stock Photo: Odyssey-Images (b). 47 Alamy Stock Photo: INTERFOTO (crb); Odyssey-Images (t). 48 Alamy Stock Photo: Photo 12 (clb). Getty Images: MPI (c); ullstein bild (cr). 49 Alamy Stock Photo: Lebrecht Music and Arts Photo Library (cr). Getty Images: Chicago History Museum (cl); ullstein bild (b). 50 123RF.com: sabphoto (cr) Alamy Stock Photo: Glasshouse Images (crb); Granger Historical Picture Archive (cra). Getty Images: ullstein bild (cl). 51 Alamy Stock Photo: Ed Buziak (bc); Granger Historical Picture Archive (tr/Owen); Everett Collection Inc (br). Dorling Kindersley. Dreamstime.com: Sergii Moskaliuk/Seregam (tr). Getty Images: whitemay (clb). 52–53 Alamy Stock Photo: Everett Collection Inc (t). 52 Alamy Stock Photo: Trinity Mirror/Mirrorpix (br); Science History Images (cl) 53 Getty Images: Bettmann (crb); Hulton Archive (cra) 54–55 Getty Images: Bettmann (b); Hulton Deutsch (t). 55 Alamy Stock Photo: Heritage Image Partnership Ltd (cb). 56 Alamy Stock Photo: Maurice Savage (b); Shawn Hempel (tr). 57 123RF.com: Scott Fensome/zollster (cl). Alamy Stock Photo: Richard Levine (tr). Getty Images: Katie Garrod (b). 58 Getty Images: Arterra (cl). 58–59 Dorling Kindersley: The Tank Museum (c). 60 Alamy Stock Photo: Science History Images (bl). Dorling Kindersley: Royal Museum of the Armed Forces and of Military History, Brussels, Belgium (tl). 61 123RF.com: Scott Fensome/zollster (tc). 62 Dorling Kindersley: Royal Airforce Museum, London (Hendon) (tl). 64 123RF.com: Photography (tl).

Endpaper images: Front: Alamy Stock Photo: David Coleman cl, Granger Historical Picture Archive cla, Alan Pembleton crb; Dreamstime.com: Lilyforman bc (flag); Getty Images: JEAN-CHRISTOPHE VERHAEGEN bl; Back: Alamy Stock Photo: Glasshouse Images clb, Granger Historical Picture Archive cra, Keystone Pictures USA bc, Keystone Pictures USA crb, World History Archive c; Dorling Kindersley: John Pearce cb; Dreamstime.com: Engin Korkmaz/Hypnocreative ca, Eq Roy tc; Getty Images: Henry Guttmann cla.

Cover images: Front: Alamy Stock Photo: Trinity Mirror Mirrorpix tr; Dorling Kindersley: Imperial War Museum, London bc, John Pearce crb, Jean-Pierre Verney cr, Collection of Jean-Pierre Verney bl, Collection of Jean-Pierre Verney bl/(morphine); Back: Dorling Kindersley: Jean-Pierre Verney By kind permission of The Trustees of the Imperial War Museum, London cr; Front Flap: 123RF.com: Photography cl/(1); Dorling Kindersley: Birmingham Pals br/(1), Royal Museum of the Armed Forces and of Military History, Brussels, Belgium cr/(2), Jean-Pierre Verney cla/(1); Back Flap: Dorling Kindersley: University of Aberdeen crb/(1).

All other images © Dorling Kindersley
For further information see: www.dkimages.com

My Findout facts:

Timeline of World War I

Follow the timeline to find out when important events in World War I happened.

The Ottoman Empire (Turkey) joins the war against the Allies (Russia, France, and Britain).

Ottoman Empire coat of arms

First German airship bombing raid on London.

Zeppelin airship

The Archduke of Austria-Hungary visits Sarajevo, in Bosnia, with his wife. A Serb shoots them dead.

Germany supports Austria-Hungary. It declares war on Russia, then on France, Russia's ally.

Allies land soldiers at Gallipoli to attack the Ottoman Empire.

June 1914	July 1914	Aug 1914	Aug 1914	Oct 1914	April 1915	April 1915	May 1915	May 1915

Austria-Hungary goes to war with Serbia. Russia backs Serbia.

German armies invade Belgium to attack France. Britain declares war on Germany.

First gas attack on the Western Front is at Ypres, in Belgium.

Gas mask

German U-boat sinks British ship *Lusitania*. Of 1,198 people dead, 128 are Americans.

Central Powers

The Central Powers were Germany, led by Kaiser Wilhelm II; the Austro-Hungarian Empire; and the Ottoman Empire (Turkey). Bulgaria also joined the Central Powers.

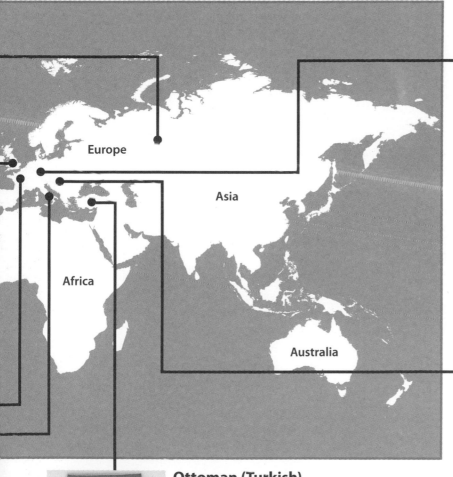

Europe

Asia

Africa

Australia

German army helmet

Germany

Generals: Paul von Hindenburg, Erich Ludendorff

Key battles: Mons (Belgium), Tannenberg (Germany), Somme (France), Spring Offensive (France and Belgium)

Total forces: 11 million

Losses: 7 million

Austro-Hungarian postage stamp

Austro-Hungarian Empire

Generals: Archdukes Albert-Friedrich and Joseph-Ferdinand

Key battles: Brusilov Offensive (Austria-Hungary), Isonzo (Austria-Hungary and Italy)

Total forces: 7.8 million

Losses: 1 million

Atatürk

Ottoman (Turkish) Empire

General: Kemal Atatürk

Key battles: Gallipoli (Turkey), Palestine, Iraq (Middle East)

Total forces: 2.8 million

Losses: 1 million

Things to find out:

....

....

....

....

....

....

....

....

....

....

....

....

....

....

....

....

....

....

....

....

World War I

Author: Brian Williams
Consultant: Simon Adams

Senior editors Marie Greenwood, Vineetha Mokkil
Art editors Rhea Gaughan, Seepiya Sahni
US editor Jenny Wilson Siklos
Project editor Ishani Nandi
Editors Anwesha Dutta, Shambhavi Thatte
Project art editor Nehal Verma
Managing editors Laura Gilbert, Alka Thakur Hazarika
Managing art editors Diane Peyton Jones,
Romi Chakraborty
Jacket designer Kartik Gera
Jacket coordinator Francesca Young
DTP designers Dheeraj Singh, Syed Mohammad Farhan
Picture researcher Nishwan Rasool
CTS manager Balwant Singh
Pre-production producer Dragana Puvacic
Production controller Isabell Schart
Art director Martin Wilson
Publisher Sarah Larter
Publishing director Sophie Mitchell
Educational consultant Jacqueline Harris

First American Edition, 2018
Published in the United States by DK Publishing
345 Hudson Street, New York, New York 10014

Published in Great Britain by Dorling Kindersley Limited.
A catalog record for this book is available
from the Library of Congress.

ISBN: 978-1-4654-6930-4 (Flexibound);
978-1-4654-7317-2 (Hardcover)
Printed and bound in Malaysia

DK books are available at special discounts when purchased
in bulk for sales promotions, premiums, fund-raising, or
educational use. For details, contact: DK Publishing Special
Markets, 345 Hudson Street, New York, New York 10014
SpecialSales@dk.com

A WORLD OF IDEAS:
SEE ALL THERE IS TO KNOW

www.dk.com

Contents

German soldier

US soldier's hat

Assassination of Franz Ferdinand

2